M000197660

SAM'S TEETH

SAM'S TEETH | PATRICK CULLITON

SUBITO PRESS 2017

Sam's Teeth © 2017 Patrick Culliton
All rights reserved.

ISBN: 978-0-9906612-7-6

Cover illustration, design & typesetting by HR Hegnauer
    www.hrhegnauer.com
Text typeset in Garamond and Grotesque

Subito Press
Department of English
University of Colorado at Boulder
226 UCB
Boulder, CO 80309-0226
subitopress.org

Distributed by Small Press Distribution
1341 Seventh Street
Berkeley, California 94710
spdbooks.org

Generous funding for this publication has been provided by the Creative
Writing Program in the Department of English and the Innovative Seed
Grant Program at the University of Colorado at Boulder.

for my Parents

HORNET HOMILY

Cow of sleep, take my arm.
Sponge me across
the sky's filthy countertop.
Close these looking balls, friend.
Force me to knit
the toothy threads of hours.
Preach to me
from your garden of paper.

Cow of sleep, unfasten this brain
belt. Turn off this pig
music. Fill the room
with fat, white quiet.
Inject me with December
and let me spread, a lake.

Overtake misfortune until melodic.
Liquid through the copper and wander
the woods cooing with numbers. Kettle
what disarms your learning
and sew a quilt of damage.

Boy, blessed is the indeed of waking.
Shiver at all the wonder. Worry it.
Dirty yourself with bicycle light.
Telephone the alpine flowers. Skinny
through the skin of this. Needle it, draw.

They sound Viking yet composed.
The sea luminesces beyond
their brave vehicles. They are recreational

and drawn in the image of a road
that leads out past questioning.
They are a sort of substance.

They are two roughed quarters placed
in the hand of a child. They are the Lord's
face asleep above the far-lit gray.

My heart is as hilly as the spoon
drawer in your kitchen. Tongue a little
whip that smites. The tickle in the back of
your throat is me. The roots gone rotten are me.
I vivacious the saloon now. I show off

my ability to shrug and let. Songs leapt
and relaxed me when we rid. May you wake,
the moon an argument on your face.
Your name is a ship
in a harbor lousy with low horns.

You look like traditional songs
in a jukebox tuned to sell crotch.

When I put you on the room
ambers. The patrons embrace, pouring

wind on each other.
The neon fixes its fidget.

Fog unwraps the city and slants
the light in, painting a Christmas

on their faces, setting their inner pinball to tilt.

Cut the gas on what makes you
announce the fires of December

Wichita your innards have become.

Swim to this other dark
where your teeth glint like almond meat

and you laugh off the cold's blue, carnivorous coat.

For us a token in the laundry room
while the mothers sleep off their wine quota.

The snowflake theory has yet to consider mutants.
Don your pie tin faceguard for the animal filmstrip.

I'm a lot like Donald Duck
when my mouth goes like this.

I whiff when dusk pitches and pass out
into your thighs, despising people
built from so much water.

If a train barreled out of your thighs
I'd wait for it to stop
and then whip the passengers

with padlocks. In the ribs
and occasional knees I'd whip them,
with cracks like luncheon ice.

Your mother's sweat mingles
with our soup and I list events
unsuitable for this family reunion

in my secret backyard.
The carpenter looks sad
when he completes the table and you

need to stop driving by his shop or
let me sit up in my seat when you do.
He might emerge from his aluminum garden.

He might start carving a canoe.

The metalhead next door gave his bird
house the business with a Louisville slugger.
I struggle with rowboat puzzles, wishing
seats for every letter. Now I see his lady won't get one.

I see she isn't map fluent, standing at the screen.
She doesn't adhere to the time limit. She's C.
I go from sympathy to wanting to bed her and back
to the passing dizzies. My glass has a slight rise

in the lip, impeding my true purpose:
to drink and rough you out a course for sleeping.
Slow red sea monsters and tilted ships.
The only fish I kept had nine hooks in its gut.

When they crowned you Miss Roadside Flowers
was your speech prepared by a hypnotist?
I apologize for not listening. I was

looking into your stomach to see what you were
conceived to and it wasn't until cupcakes after,

when you said at the interview it was a wheat field,
the only silent place besides anger.

I feel a cannonball rising in me. Root
beer belly jellied out in my singlet, hair a slick
of coils. I am buffalo sauce, I am hot wings
throwing snake dances into the nostrils of the forsaken.

Take of my body, strange woman. Tonight
we sweep out the ground floor of the piñata factory.
Our waters have plumped with revised fish.

Our Ferris wheel runs on the recitations of schoolchildren.
Flies write the state song onto sides of cattle.
Do the doggy paddle real low, do the carwash curtain.
Remove the stinger from my foot with your teeth.

Now show it to the audience. Now accept
their Kleenex money. I am hot soda, I can.
Sunburn feels good on my mouth. I have tambourines
in both armpits. I do the ruckus. I am gas.

I trap the song Waylon Jennings became as he ascended.

I signed the treaty with fish hooks,
sided with the risen knuckle, hung
a bouquet of raccoon skulls over the door,
made a rattle out of Uncle Sam's teeth

and an aspirin bottle. Of his mistresses,
I am most fair. I coat his bass drum
with Vaseline and ash. I name the stars
on his neck after yet-to-be-declared battles.

Shriek Formal, Begonia Folly, March
of the Stricken Goose. He summons
a bugle from air, clubs me on the knee,
and plays a song twice the length it takes

blood to cake to sap on skin.
His laughing ribs grind a whale song.

THE BOY WHO ASKS WHY THEY LEAVE THE SKY OFF OF MAPS

He kicks my shin when I tell him they ran out of blue ink.
What about the sun, then, and the moon, I ask. He wails.
I tell him he's free to draw his own map of the sky and he
mispronounces ridiculous. Our heads tilt on their axes as we
look at each other. Down to the floor. Back to each other.
Maybe because nobody lives there. His grandmother lives
there, many dogs. I realize how far behind I am. He starts to
bounce. I make pocket change music. Sweat rivers down my
back. The maps would be too heavy. The maps would be too
light. They'd have to make a legend for snowstorms. Because, I
don't know, because they don't know the mileage. We sit in the
question for hours. Because it only means the world to him, I
blurt I've got it, I've finally got it. That would be the part you
put pins in in order to fix the world to your wall. You can't pin
the sky. The pins would be so many birds, he says.

STOVE NOTE

I'm off to ice skate on the roofs of the wealthy.
See eight of me figuring a way to slink out.

See the smoke clouding my mouth. That's not smoke,
Mother. I don't want to die. I want to reach

a treetop. Why do you whisper into
a bottle? I have a fully functioning ear.

I'm only skating to see if graceful tastes like ice, and
I think there's a safe full of ice in this house.

I'll crash through and steal. No more
bone breaking, no more chicken skin peeling

for you. I predict parasol drinks, gulls in harmony
with spray. I'll pay to have your skin shrunken.

No more accordion arms.
I'll pay, too, to have my ears stretched

large enough to hold your hysterical.
Large like gramophone mouths. Like two amplified magnets.

No, no, like refrigerators, deep and shelfless.

ARS POETICA

Life is funny but not
like buzzards crashing a funeral.

Sunday stabs me
in the confidence.
Wallet light of ham,

I walk into who I am
and ask for a magazine
to thumb while waiting.

COMMUNION BUFFET

The tree looks peaked
from a day of meetings.

The tree longs to not long
to shake its tambourine
in a bar band.

The tree can't fight
the image of an escort,
done for the day,
slipping bills into a sock.

That money soaks but spends.

It floats in the same cloud,
badge among badges.

The tree tries to sketch
the rooster it's just a feather on.

That is its crossword puzzle.

LOUSY WITH CURRENT

I turn left like a lemon
of crows, fall
into your tuba and play
twelve bars of frog.
What do you do with winter
thunder? Patting it on
the head is disrespectful
to clouds that raised us
to be graceful,
even in the Laundromat.

Any number of things can pummel.
One window counts
steeple, oak, and Chevrolet.

I dreamt once
we were Marilyn and Joe,
right down to the walrus attack.

VACATION JOURNAL

That contrail looks like a pipe cleaner

That contrail looks like your credit score

That contrail looks like it needs another contrail
to help it check the sky for lice

That contrail looks like a thermometer
in search of the American anus

That contrail looks like nice try
whiting out death's measle-throated holler

That contrail looks like the delicate reed
in the throat of the singer alone
in a volcano of song you chose
the wrong life path

That contrail looks like you never could
draw a straight line pissant

That contrail looks like FWD: odor in administrative building

That contrail looks like clothing
with sunblock woven right in

That contrail looks like a scented trash bag full of lawn clippings

That contrail looks like I'm sorry
but happy to inform you this message has no content

That contrail looks like we're improving
our advertisements based on

That contrail looks like how we defer
loan payments and swim
naked as pine cones

That contrail looks like 40% off lifelike trees

That contrail looks like remember
when I had that panic attack
at your aunt's baptism

That contrail looks like the hum
from the hospital during a blackout

That contrail looks like the straw of Zeus too bad
he doesn't use straws he drinks
straight from the bottle like your Uncle Randy
whose divine offspring include being
a daylight dick and some Styx tapes

JIMMIE LOUIE'S BALD REMEMBRANCES

I'm like Buddy Holly and the Trix rabbit wrapped up in one. I'm a better narrator than dusk. Dusk is mostly gas, whereas I'm a heap of Greco-Roman chiseled superflesh. I rub butter on my muscles and break plates over them for hours. I brand myself and feel sorry for the iron. It runs on electricity. I don't. Birds fly into me and die.

When I played Jesus in 2nd grade Sister Mary pulled me aside, said Jesus your suffering was not believable. The Crucifixion is the third fiddle. You upset it. All of her, whip included, smelled of peanut brittle. I was into her. She played mean guitar. She said deny the horse almonds, hone your squint. The curtain flexed. We got shadows. I applauded at the applause and shot imaginary guns.

And then the Horsies threw us from our bikes. I still, over bacon, think about blowing up their gas station. But then I think it's better for them to just work their station. I'm a good kid. I think of how fat they must be now and how they smelled like a wheel skidding on a block of Swiss cheese. Then I think about blowing up their gas station again. It's a wonder I get anything done, given all of my revenge fantasies. I also sleep a lot.

My old man is paperboy emeritus of Cleveland's east side. My old man likes the smell of empty bars. My old man has a few, heads to the pet shop, and asks them to put a parrot on his shoulder. My old man can coat a house with two gallons and a stolen ladder. My old man has a hole in each hand where his brothers go. My old man grabs his tongue, milks the taste of dimes. My old man stinks of scrambled eggs and Haynes auto manuals and can kick your old man's ass.

Lisabelle's painting a portrait of me to put above the mantle, below the antlers, beside the cigar box. Who's Lisabelle? She's the one wearing my old man's work shirt backwards. It's just long enough. How a portrait? Staple me to the floor and cascade the medicines. Lisabelle's the kind of girl you'd blow your allowance on at Skee Ball to get her a green rabbit's foot, I tell my old man. Why, he says, so she can hang it on some other jagoff's rearview? My old man's working on our family's illustrated history of romantic relationships. The people look like vacuum cleaners.

The summer of love ended when the Cuyahoga River ignited. Bringing this up at the funeral home earns you a squeeze in the shoulder meat. We're not a river people. We're a drywall people. We don't visit, we fix up your homes. Without rock and roll nothing gets done. Embracing the mistake, that's what frightened the disc jockeys. Except Alan Freed. He wasn't scared of shit.

My woman makes my teeth sweat when she says bring it over here, Turnstile. I said my woman puts away the Christian. We could make a table of babies. We could eat mass McDonald's. Puffy we rub better. I said she's gonna let me with the razor later. She's plenty lemonade. My woman invented wearing a towel all day. I said she peels my head open, stuns the workers in there. The moon draws a lot of water.

I come from a long line of punches, a snuff tin filled with quarters, an arsonist grocery clerk, and a flasher. I come from Bob Golic's mullet and a van with racing stripes. I come from skin magazines in the shrubs, a lot of stealing, the drunk who took a left into the ice cream stand, and the sprinkles in the employee's wet hair. How upsetting it must be for worms after rain. Nobody likes being pounded out to the sidewalk where I come from, which is one part diving board, two parts salt breeze, and the rest lighter fluid.

At winter's onset, my uncle used to paint leaves along the stripped branches of his trees. Whenever I held the paint can for him he paid me a nickel. I still have them. I'm going to build something. A castle, maybe a cannon. I wonder if whoever I give it to won't appreciate it the way I didn't appreciate my now dead uncle who painted leaves on his trees and left his catch on the garage roof so he could study their bones onto canvas and showed me his gold ring of a loving couple in 69 and buried treasures in my yard the night before my birthdays that I still haven't found and dropped a lit book of matches into a box of fireworks at the camper and laughed and laughed drunk and puncturing our water toys yet he still got up first to make Navy eggs on a Coleman grill that he made into a turtle for my Confirmation that I still talk to when I'm too ripped to enter our cold house.

I hold football games in the small field of my hands. You think I'm praying. Who yells *tackle that son of a bitch!* at a prayer? The only similarities between my prayers and the players in my hands is they both march out of the tunnel wearing shiny helmets and look slap-faced at the crowd.

You should see this photo of my old man talking on the phone. It's from February of '73. He's trying to call my sister in the womb, to warn her of the letdown. The cord tangles into a wishbone. He holds the left clavicle. I thought you should know this and that I can only see white canoes beneath his irises, that the yellow of the wall he's leaning into is eight degrees duller than the sun, and he tells the truth about pet deaths.

I hope nobody reads this and says it's "chill" like they do sometimes about music. Like, "We're gonna hang out, smoke a little weed, and listen to some chill music." I've said all kinds of floppy shit, but not that. I hope when somebody reads this it inspires them to smash a bunch of bottles into a lake, turf someone's lawn, feel bad about it, and then offer to be an oxygen tank checker at bingo. I hope this inspires some foggy sex. I hope nobody reads this and says, "I want to hang out with this guy. I bet he's got some stories." I don't want to hang out with you. I hate stories. You should see how I treat library books.

I am the My Little Pony in your hand. You use the sparkle comb on me. Each stroke feels like coasting down a steep hill. Then you push my face into another My Little Pony's face. Then you bind us at the neck with a bracelet. Then you drop your hand and make the universal bomb crashing sound. Then you cackle and rub your nose at the same time like a squirrel my brother brains with a pellet gun.

I spend ten minutes wondering what words the wound has for the knife. What confuses me is that my knives just sit there like nutcrackers. My wounds, however, form two lines and play Red Rover, Red Rover. For my wounds to play all I need to do is lie around like a liquored up uncle. To get my knives to interact, though, *I* need to be all determined and shit. I will lie with my knives *and* my wounds while it snows like a raffle drum. I was saying earlier how great it would be, snow. Look at me getting what I want and enjoying it.

SONG

Emma is your brain ok did it
slip. The sky has a bunch
of stupid potions. Now your chin

will fit a starling keep it in there
post-stitch. We can sew stars on the fog
house for work. Is your brain

ok Emma did you break a heel
did it slip. It's ok to never
forgive ice its stupid potions.

Quiet Emma
Chicago is quiet with alert
little lights and half-rain.

BRINE

My boot blabs at

the ground and I get nearer
that cloud stretching
its quadriceps beyond
the oil well
that looks like an amusement
park ride as it fucks the ground.
We are pearls curled fetal in the wash.
I once shampooed a pelican with dawn
is a sentence more than one of us

utters around a fire
before a gulf blubbers up
her throat. How unlike ocean
a finger looks to the nape.

STOP IT CROWN

Captain dust, captain duet,
captain dulcimer, dull captain

biffing through the curtain.   Lights!

America, the dead won't change

you. It's you. You change
them with each swallow. Your tail gets
smellier, a standard falls from your forehead.

Dip a claw into the promised land
while my anxiety reanimates
every taxidermied beast.

United States of tentacle,
triplet the snow off your boots.
I have a taste for glass.

We try to chart
where heartache falls on the food chain.

This is hilarious to horses.
They rear out of the
stall into night's purple program

laughing at how we take
stars as instruction to seek
out a bed, to sleep not
standing up like
understudies for the dead.

Remember how we hated disco/
weren't born yet? Best train the fright,
freeze it on speed dial.

Don't think in a pictograph that pits
the heart beside a red rubber coin purse
unless you want permanent dyspepsia.

We can only sail to America via doubt
in any engine other than the tongue.
Just ask farms. They'll be there,

manufacturing our shared nightmare.
When we have sex we're a thresher

separating a kernel so small the sun
can't reach it with her sword.

A temporary morgue
was set up somewhere
on the school grounds.

Now is not the time
to talk about what red
glows from the attic.

A hand shouldn't explode.
Cheap Trick shouldn't come on.

Nobody should wake up
covered in disease.

In fall, most sincere form of money,
we tent out in fatass dark.
Our teeth flash
like America's ghost
meat and we forgot
to pay the water
bill. You're right.

We shouldn't pony
up for anything that governs
more than half our body
when in supervised woods
we can name the hurricanes
on our thumbs, issue
as a warning a Cadillac.

I have 5+ years spirit analysis,
America. I'm fluent

in the berries
of concern. Sip

my juices. I bring
you an ethic

of uncertainty, palpitations
be named. I make good

brick, good wheel.
I'm trained to be silent

as a jet. I remain
sensitive to your watercolor blood

portraits. We're a good
fit, a bulldozer in a sink.

A friend visits and we nap,
hoping for a storm to loosen
our sinuses enough

to snort the theories
off America's mantle.
I'm a cage on the prow.

Stick a candle in me.
I can't see my love's outline
between the foam and the dead.

What's the use in a nest, love,
in this palace of fine particulates?

In America we won't repeat ourselves
on the long drive from nowhere to nowhere.

Admission will be lightning dust
over corn fields in Rogue's Hollow.

I don't want to be an amplifier in cutoffs
anymore, love. I don't want to house

heaps of lag bolts in my body.
I don't want the dead to cut wakes
through my sleep or anything you're beside.

I will rim the bomb's nose with soap.
I will rope the dead in closer and feel for
their torches because I'm useless.

When the dead think of America
they lose their stench.
Oh scentless skeletons,

when my love thinks of America, does she
have new arms, flexible as stems? Flowers. Ugh.

When flowers think of America
they get performance anxiety.

When Paul Simon thinks of America
he slips a matchstick into his mouth,

stares out over Central Park, and sees
an acoustic sex act.
When Tony Soprano thinks of America

he hears the dread quack quack.
When my soul thinks of America

it becomes Dan Dierdorf broadcasting a fever dream.
When handguns think of America

they sing the number song.
1, 2, 3, 4, 5, when Lincoln thinks of America
does he turn to verse?

Probably not. He probably walks the root
system of an oak, silvering up the leaves

like a typewriter thinking of America
that taps ampersands in a line

off the margin and into infinity,
which is always to your right,

where someone
more beautiful than you should be,
looking you in the eye
but thinking of herons.

I get chased through a warehouse
by goons, led to an orange
door that says "Lenny Bruce's Grave"
but then I smell your armpits in the kitchen

and feel safe. Everything we've saved
will vaporize upon entry
so let's give it away, save Ohio.

Let's hold Ohio close to our chests
and throw stiff arms into the atmosphere.

I swim in a foot

of snow, my wicked face
out of your mind

because you're thinking about Tammy
Wynette keeping her beautician's license

up to date no matter her
fame. It's that act

I want as our flag,
not 6:14 in the morning

when the sun spins up, salami
god of our collective liver.

I remember when the Mansons murdered the Cleavers.
We were a song stuck in a teenager

rubbed to scratching by that terrible fabric.

I can't wait to rent the crawlspace
above America. No more facsimile weapons
in the excuse biscuit,
no bullets in the food pyramid.

All fall down. All crawl.
All claw at the mistreated dirt.
Some say the one about America is all build up.
It wouldn't be if we worked

a little more tongue into our kisses.
I'm ashamed of the way we kiss America.
If eulogies were a tongue

kiss, we'd be there already,
painting its broad side with kerosene soaked brooms
until it erupts like discovering

a piece of bone in an andouille link.

TALL SKELETON

I'm a good liver.
Are you a good liver?
Let's be good livers.
Let's be a supreme of livers.
A puddle of livers in the morning.
Livers in the limitless noon.
Bonnie is a liver. Michael, too.
If the sea turns to chalk, livers.

When it snows teeth

let's be supreme a truck of livers.
A bounding sailbus of livers.
A stout holiday of livers.
Let's promise the seal with moss, livers.
Cast off your spiral, liver. Erect a hula.
Duck, liver, the non's arrow
until the swan lifts its horn.

ON STILTS

Gowns of green snow
film my pitcher.

I drink mute, separating
the angel out of me

like a shoulder. Chained
mutt, choir of anger,

Giovanni the baker,
step forward and point

me to water.
I'm an ice-bedraggled pack mule,

this collar of bells
the only clamor proof my dead

still produce sound.

BLOODY MARY

There's a trace of piss in everything. Let's party.
You're supposed to hold your breath while you sink,
as a way of not imitating the dead at all.
The dead don't wonder
what bottom lies beneath another.

The dead don't cry
at a rerun of *Cheers*
in the corner of a hospital cafeteria.
The dead don't dislike their haircut or salad spinners.
I remain in liquid.

I spend the average American work day
worrying about a routine checkup.

The dead don't do that but I do because of the dead
and pools and my love of carbonation
and how a song can bring Nicole
two barns down from Gemini.

I saw a monarch this morning. It was fine.
I washed the car for some reason.

JACKKNIFE

I watch a bird nest
in the second
O in Amoco
and the head
of a comet screaming
from the lifeguard's left hip.

Facts, like goggles,
take a little spit,
still slip and fog.
The key, I tell myself,
is toss thought
and find your form
not before the impact but at,

like walking to the stereo
at the end of the hall
when your friends start
talking about that Žižek guy.

FIGURE FOUR

My allusions lead to a hardware store.
The saw aisle, one over from the nails.
One of the ones that also sells
bikes and flat pop.

Never give this place your number.
Never ask them how they know your name
when they ask, "are you alright,
your name?" after you run

into the broken automatic door,
forget what part
of me you came to replace,
and buy an envelope of seeds

SAILOR DIVE

After you left I went under
water, guided by the week
old bar of soap moon,

a hammer
to remove the apostrophe.

MY BOOK REPORT ON THE AFTERLIFE

There is a creek in Euclid

called crayfish chorus.

I know that pudding water

better than I do my sister.

My body, caution tape

in a cemetery that it

is, publishes a magazine

on the bonesad as it sets in

during the stupid part of summer

when Bush plays the river

bend. Peanut vendors

laminated with sweat.

You've seen a hose

loll with potato bugs and perk

at the nozzle's turning, yes?

It's like that with its shirt on

inside out. I have pall bearer anxiety. What

with my hand condition. I did my book report

on the afterlife. It's an endless bank,

every teller's face consommé.

Now I sit in the surf with Chris

until a red moon slips out and sinks us

down to the good sand they

make into hospital bricks.

Grandpa was a traveling mirror

salesman. He'd knock and hold them

before his body.

If the customer did

a double take or laughed

it was top shelf, ribs, and strange

that night. He had his casket lined

with pockets. He wore red suits

in black and white photos.

When it set in, MoMo said

it's humid as dicks on turkey day.

Tony Pepperoni whispered

through the grape fence: I taste lightning.

Turn your bikes upside down.

Then run.

May we all snap like sausages done right.

May emergency broadcasts interrupt Aerosmith

forevermore. Show me one flashlight

that isn't fumbled for. File into the hall,

fall on your knees, cover your head.

Imagine peanut butter,

the creaming of your house.

So swim. Then sleep like ashes.

It's so quiet in my mind you can hear a hot dog

thaw off from its seven enemies.

Beautiful women sunbathe on their stomachs,

straps undid. Beautiful men, too.

It's so quiet in my mind waves turn in on themselves.

Bad shit goes down in the middle of the ocean

but not in my mind, where she never comes home

with the fruit. I had my mind clear-felled.

A deer just nuzzled an electric fence but you didn't

hear it because you're in my mind,

where telephones are never invented.

Reach me via milk.

Honey, go to the store for baking soda. Take a half hour.

Watch cattle in swelter

and grit for twenty-two

minutes. Try to walk through

the front door. See if it lets you.

It's like that with its shirt off.

Drank some paint thinner once,

took a ride to 7-Up heaven.

I got the hospital's best crib. Had

this demented frog mirror.

What you saw was its mouth.

After somersaulting in another human

being's stomach should I be

surprised by congenital letdown?

She says the uglier you are, the closer you come

to true solitude. This reminds me of the manatee's whiskers.

Even the ugliest thing ever, the manatee, mates.

I believe in one manatee twirling like a necklace,

whereas you believe in two manatees grazing

beside the power plant. We shall never meet

in conclusion, where the manatee's whiskers

fade like the ship that drifts when

my imagination can't sleep in some stranger's home.

She's the intro to "Honky Tonk Women."

Before the guitar enters. Before big Buzz

starts dancing like a backhoe

at my sister's wedding, 240 steaks in

a conga line, pissing on treetops,

and the priest's collapse during Communion.

Before Uncle Ray's apology in the hot

boxed garage for sloshing over our Christmas

tree eleven years prior. It must suck for him

to categorize everything he did with cancer

before its diagnosis. Like being handed lead

stopwatches by the boxful.

Before we took our first collaborative shower

and I helped her into fishnets.

Before the umbrella nicked MoMo's head

and everyone laughed until she fell.

Frank Booth is alive and well.

He hears crayfish scream in the grass.

All my suicides appear

on a platform behind the group,

elevated by some level hell.

They are medals I wear

at a fingernail's pace

into the sea's slack gravy.

Sometimes I hear them mushroom

from the sprays. I'm not

swimming to you, dummies.

Down in Carolina I got chopped,

slow shoulders. I got the eels.

I got started with by appleheads,

wedged into the bathroom door

like a green New Testament.

Mom always said start a fight

you're grounded. Finish it

we'll clog you with French fries.

I prefer bad thoughts.

I control the goat hammer.

They won't upset my weather experiments.

I'll find the least rained on animal.

We played shoot the sheep in the roses

while the doctors cut a railroad

in mom's chest. My brother said

I had the best aim to prevent

the waiting room spazzes.

Recovered, I got her plastic bedside cup.

"You can fill it with coins."

I wasn't that good of a son.

I mostly played oxygen

mask with it past bedtime.

Vitus, my patron saint,

is a narcoleptic lifeguard.

When the thought of being lowered balloons,

I wrap my mouth around an oak and fell it.

My sister, queen of box fans,

taught me coyote bones

tell us nothing of their mileage.

That gets stored

in the eyes, eaten first.

You can lead a hearse to water.

I'm no flat top. 7-Up and coal

bricks don't move my grease.

I live outdoors, people,

raised on tent stakes and ground chuck.

This barbecue looks like a coffin because it is.

This is what we do in light.

Then we ride dirt bikes

across the flea market grounds.

If someone wipes out the party swells.

The old man does the goose dance.

And when we find the melonheads

we'll ease them with needles,

put them in old gym uniforms,

and teach them to drive

so they can get beverage truck jobs.

Then we can start

our own rocket car business

and get tv-in-the-garage rich.

Stay nautilus in your rind

when the ocean turns to horses and

fat angels flick on like old televisions.

It's brother picking time in Florida.

I bet it feels like watching plovers

dive when they lift you up to their ears.

I bet their ears smell like pillows.

I bet their breath sounds like

bright black morning light.

Looking down, I imagine

my folks, split now, lugging

a car battery wherever

they go.

Guess your pitching speed at the church

carnival, win a two liter.

All my clairvoyant friends have diabetes,

listening to the Indians fall in alarm

clock radios, and nobody brings perch

home for months. Boats

rotting on trailers, lonesome

batter calling out to grease.

Our lake was tasered while we slept.

This up-ticks my brother's blood pressure.

He makes a basement of his house

and one of his head at the office.

He looks like paper

without a match held up to it.

I'm just trying to be thirty-three

on a humid as dicks Wednesday.

Learn how to pronounce

spaghetti already,

kids on sprung seahorses.

Pop your water wings and swim

out to our lagoon.

We have a letdown for you.

It begins in the eels.

It begins in the musk

wet docks cough up.

You say sliver I say splinter

we all say bonesad

into an unplugged box fan.

WEDNESDAY, A CRITIQUE

The earthworm is a yes
man. Split in half
it says yes. Thrown
to the lake, yes.
The cricket is an idea
man. Let it drink
it starts saying things

like no songs but in legs,
everything dies, etcetera.
Even credit cards.
Even, sharp as
this is to gum,
the carriage you think
you ride in alone.

SHINE

Birds drop, fish rise
and pines scream

like Japanese candy
on red cloth with

how the moon wipes them.
I know the bus

windows are tinted but smile
still at the walkers.

It lifts them into where
snow looks like washed newspaper.

TO AN OLD ENEMY

Elvis shot his television
because the ocean in it boiled.
I hate beauty, too.

That's life in the just
typed my password
wrong feeling. I vacuumed

the creekside with your sister
twenty years ago today.
She tasted like breakfast

oranges telling me how you wept
like a placemat the night
you punched me on someone else's orders.

CUTTHROAT

for Levon

A creed says we have more than one
father. When I wander
from Earth I see belts

lashing planets into a line.
Last night, with terrible posture,
I saw a star in a bottle

shard. I had just heard
you were dying and tried to
light a branch on fire.

How pulled water illuminates failure.
No sense covering our eyes.

We blink, simultaneously, once
a day. Then he draws the cue.

What sunlight today.
Don't say things like that.
Say what horses hear.
Talc in seawater.

Death rests in bears,
pawed in gray gauze.
They against kneeling
knee the hymn's side.

Death lasts Tennessee minutes,
cicadas locked in blue wax.

Death rips us open like an eviction
notice in December.

Death collects sticks and ties
them with twine, should you
find one spinning from the rafter.

I wish you happy hammers
now that you're a comb
missing seven

teeth in the barbicide.
Earside, my barbress cuts
half a sea from my head.

Death is a vine behind the mirror.
I'm afraid six of you

will emerge and slap me
with a sack of cold powder
when I dream we take

a metalworking class and
keep making each other small

music stands.

Enjoy salted cashews.
Death is a canoe full
of daisies and dud grenades.

Enjoy waiting for fish to kiss your brain as you doze in the
backseat.

Death is bald beneath that hat
but his heart has long hair.
Sew your heart a hat.

Enjoy every orgasm painting death's lips with our moaned out
pollen,
that lost animal language recovered

from evening evening
us into a landscape: machine tree tree machine
tree sky machine.

That we earn a third shoulder
to get upriver and fall shapeless
seems a raw deal to one
who's yet to taste the aftergas.

If I don't bellow you I become 184
boxless Kleenex before a turbine.

It's weird that animals live
in trees and just sing when you can't
sleep, and trees grow weirder
in magnificence when you cut them

open and finger their paste
in your weird bean brain

where he holds a fluorescent tube
over his head, powered by a far
off radio, and turns into the woods,
lights up and amplifies the birds.

HUSKS

It's a cruel forest and it's false
berry season so

rely like Sunday
on the tongue test.

Who am I spooning tapioca into?

An unemployed straw man,
fitful in the preacher's rolodex,
rolls over on his cot and taps out
a message to the Ys.

The mouth is a hatchery.

My side, hale
nephew of no bone,
unsplittable Gemini,

filled with radishes
in the spitting dark,
senses no you in the donation,

knows even chickens
without eyes lay eggs.

We are an anthology of husks.

Like an antelope shown
a painting of an antelope,
I just want

to find a cool source
of water and not
die today.

Nothing lands on your arm like a hand buzzer like a grasshopper.

Treat everyone like worms:
rescue them into a bed
after the downpour.

I write this from inside my whale. My heart is filled with seawater.

Our skin makes us chuckle like a king
prodigious at drawing battle plans,
and I refuse to insult force by wondering
how long it takes water to bore through slabs of rock.

Let's go to that bit of lemon rind wedged in the atlas.

My heart, pink waddler
healthy enough for sex,
tells me the watermelon secret
wags in the continental shelf.

Why don't you offer your root beer float to the moon, tenant.

The terror of quiet
suburbs at night:
clean lines, adequate light.

The flag makes slurping noises.

Most lost boats find the shore
lets them down.

Lighting a bowl full of Roman
candles makes me feel less
like a kerchief of spinach in a mannequin's tooth.

I apologized to caskets as a child.

My favorite color falls
between lime and olive
green and holy men

spit its pigments
against my brainwalls
when your tavern panties
go up like steer horns.

Much more of you to smell before aping a dock.

The carnies have come to install another spring.

A pole bean punches through
soil and salutes it.

This scrap of onion
paper's refusal
to compost is a fight song.

The ventriloquist takes her dummy nightswimming.

This robin stabbed a pizza
crust, lost it three
flaps upward, and a squirrel
ran over and ate it.

Ghosts please me.

After years in the garden
the cancer had her
pulling weeds beside her easy chair,
calling the dead down for dinner.

We set an extra place as summer deflates the trees.

Listening to your
alligator snore, I insert
a clump of stars
into your mouth
until a song comes on
sturdy enough to surf across.

A battalion of pillows storms the empty beach.

A cavalier orange
leaf falls in
the official world.

We walk like leopards into elephantine snow.